Contents

D1152515

£1.50

Published by Diabetes UK **Photography** Bill Reavell **Design** Paul Grimes
Recipes developed by Louise Blair **Activity section** Janice Meakin

The pancreas

In people with diabetes, the pancreas does not produce enough insulin, or the insulin it produces does not work properly.

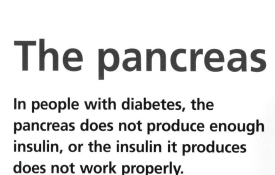

duct carrying digestive juices into the intestines

stomach

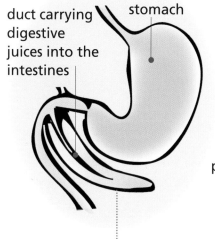

gullet

liver

pancreas

stomach

pancreas

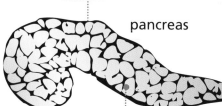

microscopic appearance of pancreatic cells

Islet of Langerhan with beta cells secreting insulin into the bloodstream

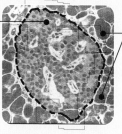

cells producing pancreatic juices

Illustration: Paul Grimes **Photography:** Blackwell Science Ltd.

What is diabetes?

Diabetes mellitus is a condition in which the amount of glucose (sugar) in the blood is too high because the body cannot use it properly. Glucose comes from the digestion of starchy foods such as bread, rice, potatoes, chapatis, yams and plantain, from sugar and other sweet foods, and from the liver which makes glucose.

Insulin is vital for life. It is a hormone produced by the pancreas, which helps the glucose to enter the cells where it is used as fuel by the body.

The main symptoms of untreated diabetes are increased thirst, going to the loo all the time - especially at night, extreme tiredness, weight loss, genital itching or regular episodes of thrush, and blurred vision.

Type 1 (insulin dependent) diabetes develops if the body is unable to produce any insulin. This type of diabetes usually appears before the age of 40. It is treated by insulin injections and diet.

Type 2 (non insulin dependent) diabetes develops when the body can still make some insulin, but not enough, or when the insulin that is produced does not work properly (known as insulin resistance). This type of diabetes usually appears in people over the age of 40, though often appears before the age of 40 in South Asian and African-Caribbean people. It is treated by diet alone or by diet and tablets or, sometimes, by diet and insulin injections.

The main aim of treatment of both types of diabetes is to achieve near normal blood glucose and blood pressure levels. This, together with a healthy lifestyle, will help to improve wellbeing and protect against long-term damage to the eyes, kidneys, nerves, heart and major arteries.

Aim of the book

This book has been designed to provide information and act as a reference for managing your weight if you have diabetes. It is not a complete guide or a comprehensive package to losing weight. It highlights the importance of weight management for people with diabetes and the relationship between blood glucose control and being overweight. It also gives practical advice on losing weight or controlling weight whether your diabetes is managed by diet alone, tablets or insulin treatment. Although there are general guidelines for weight loss, having diabetes makes two important differences. Firstly, being overweight carries more health risks in diabetes and secondly, dietary changes may affect the amount of diabetes medication you need.

> It is vital that you talk to your diabetes care team about losing weight before you start and have regular reviews of your progress.

Guide to the book

Part one Introduces diabetes and healthy living for people with diabetes.

Part two Focuses on the importance of managing your weight if you have diabetes and the relationship between blood glucose control and being overweight.

Part three Looks at meal planning and includes ways to reduce your calorie intake, helpful tips for adapting cooking methods, shopping, understanding food labels and eating out.

Part four Is divided into five recipe sections :- Breakfasts, light meals, main meals, desserts and snacks with recipe ideas and facts to help you to make changes to your eating habits and food choices with a view to managing your weight more easily.

All of the recipes are designed to be low in fat and calories. The quantities used are generally based on one or two servings, although can be easily increased to cater for more. We have included serving suggestions to help you to make balanced meals using these recipes. Individual energy requirements will vary. People who lead energetic lives or for those who are trying to maintain their weight, can increase the amount of starchy food with their meal.

Part five Gives suggested menus for different lifestyles.

Part one

Healthy eating

The diet for diabetes is the same healthy diet recommended for everyone – low in fat, salt and sugar with meals based on starchy foods and plenty of fruit and vegetables. Eating a healthy diet means balancing your food choices – it's not just about eating diet or healthy foods. You should enjoy a wide variety of foods as part of your healthy diet.

Six steps to eating a healthy diet

1 Eat regular meals based on starchy foods such as bread, pasta, chapatis, potatoes, rice and cereals. This will help you to control blood glucose levels.

2 Try to cut down on the fat you eat, particularly saturated fats as this type of fat is linked to heart disease. Eating less fat and fatty foods will also help you to lose weight.

3 Eat more fruit and vegetables – aim for at least five portions a day to provide you with vitamins and fibre as well as helping to balance your overall diet.

4 Cut down on sugar and sugary foods. This does not mean you need to try to eat a sugar free diet. Sugar can be used as an ingredient in foods and in baking as part of a healthy diet.

5 Use less salt. Try flavouring foods with herbs and spices rather than adding salt to food.

6 Drink alcohol in moderation only - that's 2 units of alcohol per day for a woman and 3 units per day for a man.

Low GI foods

Fruit apples, apricots, cherries, grapefruit, oranges, peaches, pears

Vegetables sweet potato, sweetcorn

Pulses peas, chick peas, butter beans, kidney beans, baked beans, lentils

Pasta

Wholegrains barley, bulgar wheat, Basmati rice, plain popcorn, oatmeal

Breakfast cereals porridge, Allbran, muesli

Dairy milk, yogurt

Breads pumpernickel or rye bread, pitta bread, fruit loaf

Glycaemic index

The glycaemic index (GI) is a ranking of individual foods according to the effect they have on blood glucose levels. Carbohydrate foods with a low GI cause a slow steady rise in blood glucose levels. High GI foods cause blood glucose levels to rise quickly - this is because they are digested and absorbed more rapidly. For example the GI of glucose is 100 whereas the GI of baked beans is 48. Even though you may not have heard the term GI before, you may already have been encouraged to include low GI foods such as pasta and pulses in your diet.

You can't tell a low GI food just by looking at it – and GI is not just related to the fibre or sugar content of a food. The effect of a meal or snack on blood glucose levels is influenced by many things. For example, the way in which a food is cooked and prepared, the combination of foods you eat with it and their fat and protein content as well as other foods you have eaten that day, can all have a bearing on its GI.

There is more to eating a healthy diet than just eating low GI foods – a food is not good or bad because of its GI. It is neither necessary, nor practical to look at specific GI values for every food you eat. However, including more low GI foods in your meals can help to improve blood glucose control and will help curb your appetite by making you feel fuller for longer, so you are less likely to overeat.

A question of carbohydrate

Starchy carbohydrates should form the basis of all meals – gone are the days when people with diabetes were advised to restrict these foods. Many people wrongly think that starchy foods are fattening. Although different carbohydrate foods have different effects on blood glucose levels (see *Low GI foods* on page 7), all starchy foods provide you with energy, fibre and some vitamins and are therefore an important part of healthy eating. Starchy foods are filling so basing meals on them means you can reduce the amount of high fat foods like cheese and fatty meat.

Some people with diabetes are advised to eat snacks between meals and at bed time in order to spread carbohydrate intake more evenly over the day. This can help you to control your blood glucose levels more easily. Snack foods can be high in fat and calories, so look at our snack section on page 88 for lower fat ideas.

'Diabetic' foods

'Diabetic' foods are not recommended. They still contain the same amount of fat and calories as standard foods. Diabetic foods contain alternative sweeteners to sugar such as sorbitol and isomalt. These types of sweeteners are called nutritive or bulk sweeteners and they do not provide any special benefit to people with diabetes. They still contain calories and still affect blood glucose levels.

Intense sweeteners

Intense or artificial sweeteners that are sugar free and virtually calorie free, include aspartame, saccharin, cyclamate or acesulfame K. They can be used to sweeten drinks and sprinkle on stewed fruit or cereals, but are not recommended in baking as they don't contain bulk.

For more information on sweeteners, see our *Sweetener guide* (£2.00). To order see page 102.

Part two

Weight management and diabetes

Being overweight increases the risk of developing Type 2 diabetes. This is because there is a direct relationship between being overweight and the ability to convert glucose into energy. Four out of every five people diagnosed with Type 2 diabetes are overweight. Diabetes is on the increase and one of the reasons is the increase in the number of people who are overweight.

Managing your weight (sensible slimming)

Your overall weight shows whether you are eating the right amount of food for you. If you are overweight, losing weight will help you to control your blood glucose levels more easily by reducing your body's resistance to insulin and it will help you control high blood pressure. Research has shown that good blood glucose control and good blood pressure control can reduce the risk of long-term complications for people with diabetes.

Raised blood fats (cholesterol and triglycerides) and raised blood pressure are independent risk factors for coronary heart disease and stroke. Making healthy changes to your diet like reducing your saturated fat intake and increasing your fruit and vegetable intake, in addition to controlling your weight, will help reduce blood fat levels.

Make small changes that you can stick to. Think about your usual eating habits, compare them with the six steps to a healthy diet on page 6 and see what changes you can make . Set yourself realistic targets. Start by making small changes that will easily fit into your lifestyle and maintain them. For example, cut out those extra biscuits or use a lower fat milk, eg semi-skimmed instead of full cream milk **on an everyday basis**.

Even if you don't manage to get to your ideal weight, a small weight loss will help you if you keep it off. Weight loss from a combination of increased activity and a reduction in calories is easier to achieve and maintain than a crash diet, and has benefits on overall health.

Benefits of combining weight loss and physical activity

- Helps control blood glucose levels by reducing the body's resistance to insulin.

- Reduces the risk of heart disease and stroke by improving fitness of the heart and circulation.

- Helps to lower blood fats (cholesterol and triglycerides).

- Lowers blood pressure. Good control has been proven to reduce the risk of long-term complications.

- Improves mobility, flexibility and strength.

- Reduces tiredness.

- Increases energy levels.

- Reduces joint damage.

- Relieves stress.

- Improves self-esteem.

What is the right weight?

Losing weight does not mean you have to starve. If you are not overweight at the moment, it is important not to gain weight in the future. Because we are all different shapes and sizes, it is important to decide what the healthy weight is for you. There are several ways of finding out what is right for you – talk to your diabetes care team about you and your right weight.

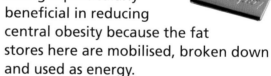

Waist circumference

Where you carry extra weight is just as important as how much. Excess fat around the stomach is particularly harmful and can increase the risk of complications linked with diabetes. This is because fat around the stomach is associated with insulin resistance, raised cholesterol and triglycerides. Physical activity combined with healthy eating is particularly beneficial in reducing central obesity because the fat stores here are mobilised, broken down and used as energy.

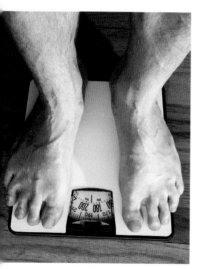

Work out if you have excess central fat by measuring your waist with a tape measure at the mid-point between the top of your hipbone and your lowest rib. If it measures more than 80cm (32 inches) for a woman, or more than 94cm (37 inches) for a man then try not to gain any more weight. If it measures more than 88cm (35 inches) for a woman, or more than 102cm (41 inches) for a man, try to lose weight.

Body Mass Index (BMI)

Your weight is often calculated as BMI which expresses adult weight in relation to height. From this you will be advised if you need to lose weight to help control your diabetes. Your GP will record your BMI in your notes.

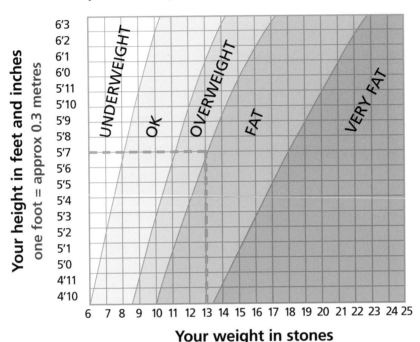

Your height in feet and inches
one foot = approx 0.3 metres

UNDERWEIGHT · OK · OVERWEIGHT · FAT · VERY FAT

Your weight in stones
one pound = approx 0.45 kilograms

To calculate your BMI: $\text{BMI} = \dfrac{\text{weight (kg)}}{\text{height (m)}^2}$

A BMI of 20-25 is classed as a healthy weight (see the chart above). You do not need to lose weight.

A BMI of 25-30 is classed as overweight. The health risks for those in this range are associated with the extra weight being carried around your middle.

A BMI greater than 30 is associated with significantly increased health risks.

Losing weight, medication and diabetes control

Talk to your diabetes care team about your medication if you are trying to lose weight. You may need to adjust the dosage of your medication as your weight changes. This is a good time to review your medication.

For example, if you are on insulin or tablets your diabetes care team may suggest reducing your dose as you are eating less. This in turn will minimise the risk of having a hypo (hypoglycaemia). Additionally, some tablets like sulphonylureas (Glibenclamide or Gliclazide) may not be the best choice of tablet if you are trying to lose weight as they tend to promote weight gain. If you are trying to lose weight, your diabetes care team may think that Metformin and the new Glitazones may be more appropriate.

Having diabetes doesn't make a great deal of difference to how you lose weight. You either have to cut down on the amount of energy (or calories) that you eat, burn off more energy by increasing your level of activity, or ideally, both. The challenge is to control your blood glucose levels as well as cut down on calories, so it is essential to monitor your diabetes control regularly. However you manage your diabetes and whoever you look to for support on weight control, it is essential that you discuss your individual needs with your diabetes care team.

If you are trying to lose weight, make sure your practice nurse, diabetes specialist nurse, state registered dietitian or GP knows.

Weighing up the benefits

Hopes of losing a lot of weight can be easily dashed after the initial enthusiasm has worn off. It is better to lose a modest amount of weight and maintain that loss, than to lose a large amount and regain it.

Most people lose a bit of weight when they first start to make changes to their eating habits. This is water to begin with. To lose fat you need to lose a steady amount of weight, in the region of 0.5kg-1kg (1-2lbs) each week at the most. If you cut down on food too drastically you lose lean muscle tissue rather than fat and also risk missing out on other vital nutrients like vitamins and minerals. To lose the recommended 0.5kg-1kg (1-2lbs) per week you need to eat about 500 calories less each day.

Physical activity benefits everyone. No matter how unfit you feel, there are ways to increase your fitness. If you have been inactive for a long time, you should consult your doctor before starting any strenuous activity. However, strenuous activity is not necessary to achieve health benefits: moderate activities such as walking briskly will not tax you unduly and you can always slow down. See the chart on page 17 to work out how to do 300-500 calorie-burning activity a day.

Follow the steps below to make small changes to your activity levels. These will greatly benefit your fitness and health. Before starting a new activity or if you have any of the complications of diabetes consult your doctor, who will be able to reassure you and help you identify the types of activity which will suit you.

Six ways to increase your energy levels

1 Walk whenever possible. Leave the car and bus and feel the difference in your legs as well as your pocket.

2 Add activity to your leisure time.

3 Be active with friends and family.

4 Use the stairs instead of lifts or escalators.

5 Try different activities to find those that suit you, short activities all count towards the aim of 30 minutes a day.

6 Commit yourself and make time, not excuses.

Activity values

If you are already doing all the six steps above and would like to increase your activity levels further, see the information below to choose activities which are effective at using calories.

Calorie-burning values of activities

Activity	kcal per 20 minutes	
Running	240	These estimates are based on a person of 68kg (10 ½ stone). They assume a continuous rate of activity. For best results, try a minimum of 20 minutes to begin with accompanied by a five minute warm-up and five minute cool down.
Swimming	200	
Dancing	200	
Cycling	160	
Brisk walking	140	
Tennis	160	
Gardening	120	
Cleaning	80	

Measured progress

Any activity will help you with your weight management and general fitness. Likewise, the more time you spend on an activity, the more calories you will burn.

However, as you increase the intensity or time, there is increased risk of injury which can outweigh the extra benefits - doing too much is not good for you.

Build up to and keep to the 'maximum benefit' zone, doing only what you feel comfortable with and increasing the length of your activities slowly.

Use the graph below to find the maximum health benefits.

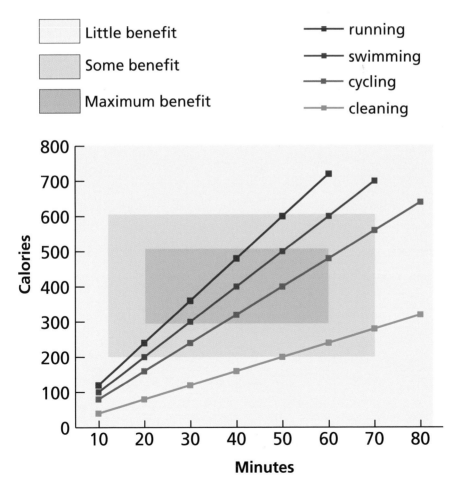

Little benefit

Some benefit

Maximum benefit

—■— running

—■— swimming

—■— cycling

—■— cleaning

Mobility, stamina and strength

Physical activity is not just about burning calories. Any activity which burns calories, also improves your strength, stamina and mobility.

Strength of your muscles protects your skeleton, organs and joints.

Stamina trains your heart muscles. A strong heart improves your circulation and copes better with times of extra energy output and stressful situations.

Mobility of joints and flexibility of your muscles allows a full range of movement, making everyday actions such as bending and stretching easier.

Aim to do a combination of activities from the chart below to achieve at least 7 x **strength** 14 x stamina 7 x **mobility** a week.

A winning combination

Activity 30 mins of:	Strength	Stamina	Mobility
Brisk walking	●	● ●	●
Gardening	● ●	● ●	● ●
Running: medium	● ●	● ● ●	●
Cleaning	● ●	●	● ●
Stair-climbing	●	● ● ●	●
Swimming: crawl	● ●	● ● ●	● ●
Swimming: breaststroke	● ●	● ●	● ● ●
Cycling: medium	● ● ●	● ● ●	●
Yoga	●	●	● ● ●
Dancing	●	● ●	●
Golf	●	● ●	● ●
Table tennis	●	● ●	●

Intensity needed to achieve total fitness

- •   easily carry and use own body weight
- ••   use and carry tools and equipment; work against resistance
- •••   lift objects or weights repetitively
- •   breathing comfortably but deeper than at rest (0-5 kcal/min)
- ••   breathing rapidly but easily able to talk (5-8 kcal/min)
- •••   breathing very fast, able to say a few words (8+ kcal/min)
- •   sitting, standing, stretching up easily
- ••   large arm and leg movements
- •••   very mobile, including spinal movements

Be active, be safe

Follow these six tips and prevent accidents and injuries:

1 Be aware of hypos. Excercise generally lowers blood glucose levels so always carry a snack (and sugary drink) and medical information.

2 If you have Type 1 diabetes or Type 2 diabetes controlled with insulin, check your blood glucose level before doing any exercise. If it is high do not exercise until it has come down. Hyperglycaemia means that there is unlikely to be enough insulin circulating to ensure uptake of glucose by the muscles and ketoacidosis may occur.

3 Let someone know where and how long you are going to be.

4 Warm up by starting slowly, and cool down by finishing slowly.

5 Wear reflective clothing at night.

6 When you have finished, stretch gently, check your feet for blisters or other injury and monitor your blood glucose levels.

> After exercising, low blood glucose levels are quite usual as the muscles replenish their stores of glucose. In fact you may be at risk of a hypo up to 36 hours after exercising. Make sure that you check your blood glucose level regularly and have a snack if necessary.

Part three

Meal planning

There is no such thing as healthy or unhealthy food. The important thing is to enjoy a variety of different foods which make up a healthy diet.

You may be trying to fit in eating with friends and family and doing more exercise, with making healthy diet changes and keeping your diabetes under control. Try to get specific advice and support from your state registered dietitian at the hospital or surgery. You may find that you need additional support from a weight management group – again ask your state registered dietitian for advice as s/he may run a group at the local clinic or be able to recommend one.

Changes to your diet

Start by taking a good look at your current eating habits. It is often easy to forget what you actually eat over the course of each day.

Step 1 - take a look at your snacks
If you have diabetes, particularly if you are treated by insulin or sulphonylureas, it is important to spread your carbohydrate intake out over the day through regular meals and snacks, helping to stabilise your blood glucose control.

In practice doing this means, choosing low fat foods and being careful about how much food you eat in total throughout the day . Eating snacks does not mean you have to increase your calorie intake - snacks should be based on carbohydrate.

Healthier snacks

Replace this	With this
Slice fruit cake	Slice of malt loaf
Packet of crisps	Popcorn
Full fat yogurt	Low fat yogurt
Cheese/crackers	Fruit bun
2 digestives	Apple
2 small samosas	banana

Think about why you are snacking. If it is because you are hungry, try filling up on low calorie options (see page 88). If, on the other hand, you are increasing your activity levels you will want to look for snacks high in carbohydrate to keep your energy levels up, but still low in fat.

If you are stepping up your activity levels, you may need to re-consider the way you plan meals and include more snacks into your diet.

There is the possibility of adjusting your medication in order to keep good blood glucose levels and avoid having a lot of extra snacks and therefore additional calories.

Whatever your reason for snacking, talk to your diabetes care team about your own needs for an approach that will suit you best.

Step 2 - take a look at your plate

The best way to cut down on calories when you are trying to lose weight is to cut down on fats, without reducing your carbohydrate intake. Fats are the most calorie dense foods we eat and cutting down on saturated fat has been shown to lower cholesterol and triglceride levels.

Use your plate as a rough guide to the recommended proportions to eat.

The idea is that even if you eat the same total amount of food during the day, by shifting the balance of what you eat so that most of the plate is covered with vegetables and starchy food you end up eating less fat and fewer calories.

So, fill half the plate with vegetables. In the other half, fill two-thirds with starchy foods like rice, pasta and potatoes and fill the final third with low fat protein foods like lean meat, fish, beans or vegetarian protein source like quorn or tofu.

A day's meal plan should include regular meals based on starchy carbohydrate foods like bread, cereals, potatoes, rice and pasta. One example would be to start the day with a breakfast of fruit, cereal with skimmed or semi-skimmed milk. Then have a sandwich for your light meal using low fat spread, a lean filling and fruit or low fat yogurt. Balance your main meal using the plate model as a guide. Fill up on vegetables at meal times and use fruit as low calorie snacks or desserts.

> Serve plenty of vegetables and salad with your meals – or fruit, in the case of breakfast.

Slash the fat

Replace this	With this	And save this (calories)
Full cream milk	Semi-skimmed milk	100 per half-pint
Double cream	Half fat fromage frais	40 per tbsp
Bag of crisps	Piece of fruit	100 per serving
2 digestives	2 gingernuts	40 per biscuit
Fried chips	Oven chips	45 per portion
Chicken breast	Skinless chicken breast	45 per portion
Cheddar	Reduced fat cheddar	60 per 40g/1.5oz
Margarine	Low fat spread	50 per 10g serving
Potatoes roasted	Dry roasted potatoes	45 per portion
Mayonnaise	Reduced fat mayonnaise	75 per tbsp
Mince	Lean mince	50 per portion
Ice-cream	Low fat yogurt	95 per portion
Fried egg	Poached egg	30 per egg

Practical tips

- **Grill, bake, poach, steam, dry roast or dry fry** foods rather than frying them, or adding fat.

- **Roast potatoes** - parboil or microwave first, then brush with a little oil and crisp them in the oven.

- **Mince or meat for casseroles** - dry fry and drain off any excess fat before adding the remaining ingredients.

- **Use pulses** such as beans and lentils to replace some of the meat in some recipes, eg casseroles. They are also good added to soups or salads.

- **Butter or margarine** - don't add to anything that isn't essential. Try using a low fat spread. It will contain less fat and therefore fewer calories than either butter or margarine.

- **Monounsaturated fats or oils,** eg olive and rapeseed or **polyunsaturated fats or oils,** eg sunflower are still 100% fat. Use them sparingly. Measure out any oil with a measuring spoon.

- **Sauces** – use cornflour or sauce flour and water to make a paste instead of blending flour and fat for a roux.

- **Cheese** – use grated cheese for sandwiches and jacket potatoes – it goes further than sliced. Cheeses such as mature cheddar or parmesan have a strong flavour so you can use less of them or try reduced fat cheeses.

Slimming foods

There are a number of products on the market which claim to help you lose weight. They may come in the form of bulking agents (fibre tablets) that are supposed to fill you up so you eat less, or diuretics (tablets that make you lose extra fluid) which may cause temporary weight loss but are not recommended.

There are meal replacements in the shape of drinks like milkshakes and meal replacement bars. These products contain a set amount of calories and nutrients and are intended to replace a meal each day – as a way of controlling calorie intake. These offer no benefit as you will not have changed your eating habits in the long-term.

There are low calorie meals which are lower calorie versions of ready made foods available in supermarkets – again the idea is to control calorie intake for you. These may be useful but you will probably need to eat more vegetables and bread with them to make them balanced meals.

Very low calorie diets

There are liquid diets which are used to replace food intake completely and which are based on very low calorie levels of between 400-800 kcal per day. These diets, such as the Cambridge diet, are usually taken in liquid form. Initial weight loss is rapid and is accounted for by loss of fluid and muscle rather than fat. This type of diet does not encourage people to make healthy changes to their eating patterns long term. These diets are only recommended under strict medical management.

Long-term healthy changes are recommended to maintain good blood glucose control, to help maintain normal cholesterol and triglyceride levels and provide a balanced diet. Whatever strategy you use – in the end you need to be able to apply it to your usual eating habits and food choice in order to maintain the changes to your diet.

The main thing to remember is that when you make changes they have to be realistic and achievable in the long-term in order to get results. Small changes are all that's needed, as long as you stick to them. You don't have to starve to get the results you want.

Shopping tips

- Choose lower fat dairy products like skimmed or semi-skimmed milk, low fat or 'diet' yogurts. Light crème fraîche and fromage frais are lower fat alternatives to cream. Remember that virtually fat free fromage frais is not heat stable whereas crème fraîche is because of its higher fat content.

- Oily fish contains more calories than white fish, but you can still include it in your diet. Choose tinned fish in tomato sauce, brine or spring water rather than any type of oil.

- Use lean meat and poultry whenever possible, removing any visible fat before cooking.

- A 15ml/1tbsp serving of French dressing or vinaigrette will add approximately 100 calories to your meal. Use a low fat or fat free dressing like one of the recipes on page 56.

- Ready-made meals and sauces tend to be high in fat and salt and low in fibre. Choose lower fat or healthy choice options as foods eaten regularly or in larger quantities, will affect your overall diet more. Vegetarian choices are not necessarily any healthier and can be high in fat. Always serve with extra veg or salad.

- Some foods do contain a lot of fat, sugar or calories but if you only eat them occasionally (eg fruit pie) or in small amounts (eg jam) then the fat, sugar and calories won't be significant in your overall diet.

Know your labels

When buying ready-meals and manufactured foods, the nutritional labelling can often help you to make healthier choices. Convenience foods can be useful as a time saving option and needn't always be unhealthy.

When comparing food labels think about how the food fits into your overall diet – how much of a food will you be eating and how often will you eat it.

- The nutrition information on the food label shows you how much of a particular nutrient (such as carbohydrate or fat) a food will provide and allows you to compare the nutrient content of foods. Information is usually given in two columns:

Use the **'per 100g'** (3½oz) column to compare the composition of similar foods, such as tins of soup.

Use the **'per serving'** column if you are comparing quite different foods, for example comparing a pizza with a tin of soup, as the weight of a serving will be different.

When using information **'per serving'** on the label, check that you are not eating a bigger serving than the size suggested.

- 'Reduced' or 'low' fat or sugar foods are lower in fat or sugar than standard versions. They can only help you reduce the fat, sugar and calories in your diet if you eat them in no greater quantities than you would ordinary versions. 'Low' as a claim means it contains less of a nutrient than 'reduced'.

Know your label

Energy • measured in calories (kcal)

the amount of energy a food gives you

to maintain a healthy weight your energy intake from food should balance your energy output from physical activity

individual requirements for weight loss will vary

the Guideline Daily Amounts (GDA) is 2500kcal for men and 2000kcal for women

Protein • measured in grams (g)

Found in meat, fish, dairy and pulses. Choose low fat versions whenever possible

most people eat more than enough protein so special guidelines aren't needed

Carbohydrate • measured in grams (g)

this includes sugars and starches

it includes natural and added sugars

of which sugars this is the amount of carbohydrate that comes from sugars

10g or more is a lot
2g or less is a little

NUTRITION
(Ty

PER 100g AS CONSUM

ENERGY

PROTEIN

CARBOHYDRATE

(of which sugars

FAT

(of which saturates

FIBRE

SODIUM

The term Guideline Daily Amount (GDA) is the figure which appears on some food labels. It gives values for average intakes of different nutrients based on average healthy adults. Individual requirements may vary.

Fat • measured in grams (g)

the total amount of fat in the food

includes saturates, polyunsaturates and monounsaturates

eat less of all types especially saturates

the Guideline Daily Amounts (GDA) is 95g for men and 70g for women

individual requirements for weight loss will vary

20g or more is a lot

3g or less is a little

Fibre • measured in grams (g)

fibre is found in fruit and veg, beans and pulses

the Guideline Daily Amounts (GDA) is 20g for men and 16g for women

3g or more is a lot

0.5g or less is a little

Sodium • measured in grams (g)

The Guideline Daily Amounts (GDA) is 2.5g for men and 2g for women

0.5g or more is a lot

0.1g or less is a little

'A lot' and 'A little' figure reproduced by permission of MAFF from Foodsense booklets Use you label (PB2362 - Crown copywrite).

...ORMATION ...es)	
	PER 25g SERVING
1560 KJ	390 KJ
367 kcal	92 kcal
7.3g	1.8g
82.7g	20.7g
8.9g	2.2g)
0.8g	0.2g
0.3g	0.1g)
3.6g	0.9g
1.1g	0.3g

Eating out

People trying to lose weight often worry about going out for fear of breaking their diet. If you eat out only on special occasions then it is not going to effect your attempts at weight loss. If you're eating out more regularly then there are ways of managing this around your diet.

Keep to one or two courses to reduce your total intake of food.

- **Starters** – choose melon/fruit/fruit juice, non creamy soups, fish and salads rather than high fat starters such as pâtés, deep fried foods with creamy dips.

- **Main courses** – choose baked or grilled meats and fish, pasta with tomato based sauces, stir-fried, and plain boiled dishes.

- **Desserts** – tend to be high in fat and calories, fruit is the obvious low calorie choice. Sorbets and ice-creams are lower in calories than gateaux and sponge puddings/pies.

- **Cheese and crackers** – cheese and butter are high in fat, so this is not a low-calorie option.

- **Try to avoid** – pastries, rich creamy sauces, deep fried dishes and butter glazed vegetables.

- **Alternative ingredients** – ask for low fat spreads and low calorie salad dressings ask for yogurt as an alternative to cream.

- **Ask your waiter** – for sauces, dressings and butter spreads to be served separately and to include generous portions of veg and salad.

Most restaurants are happy to make alterations to suit you.

Watch out
Extras can add up – chocolates/petit fours, cream, butter, second helpings, extra courses, another glass of wine/beer/liqueur.

Alcohol

If you are trying to lose weight you should cut down on alcohol. Alcohol is high in calories and also stimulates the appetite. If you are cutting down on food it is important that you do not risk going hypo (low blood sugar levels) by drinking the same amount of alcohol as usual.

Never drink on an empty stomach as alcohol increases the risk of going hypo. Low alcohol or low carbohydrate drinks offer no real benefit over ordinary alcoholic drinks. There are some low calorie alcoholic drinks available – but these still contain more calories than 'diet', 'low calorie', 'sugar free' soft drinks or water.

Being overweight increases your resistance to insulin absorption and increases the risk of heart disease, one of the complications of diabetes. Although studies have shown that alcohol in moderation can be beneficial in reducing overall risk of heart disease, alcohol is a source of extra calories which does not help your weight management.

- **The risks of being overweight will probably outweigh the benefits of alcohol.**

One 125ml glass of wine = 1 unit
1 pint ordinary strength beer or lager = 1 unit
1 pub measure of spirits = 1 unit

> If you do have an alcohol binge, eat some carbohydrate before going to bed to reduce your risk of hypoglycaemia and make sure you test your blood glucose levels.

part four

Recipes

Breakfast recipes

Often quoted as "The most important meal of the day", enjoy a carbohydrate rich start to the day. So, whether it's a bowl of cereal with low fat milk and fruit, toast and marmalade or something more formal, breakfast is not to be missed for several very good reasons:

- Research shows that breakfast eaters are likely to eat less over the whole day than breakfast skippers.

- Spreading food intake out over the day, eg three meals per day, helps to control appetite and regulate blood glucose levels.

- Breaks the night time fast, providing energy/carbohydrate to top up depleted stores.

- Is essential to balance your blood glucose levels and diabetes medication.

- Studies show people who eat breakfast are more alert and can concentrate better throughout the morning.

Banana booster drink

Serves 1

1 small banana, roughly chopped

1 x 150g carton low fat yogurt

2 teaspoons runny honey

150ml/¼ pint cold skimmed milk

Simply place all the ingredients into a food processor or blender and blend until smooth. Serve in a tall glass.

PER SERVING			
energy	protein	carbohydrate	fat
276 kcal	**13** grams	**54** grams	**2** grams

Apple and oat booster drink

Serves 1

1 small eating apple, peeled, cored and chopped

3 tablespoons muesli

2 teaspoons runny honey

200ml/⅓ pint cold skimmed milk

Simply place all the ingredients in a food processor or blender and blend until smooth. Serve at once.

PER SERVING			
energy	protein	carbohydrate	fat
288 kcal	**16** grams	**50** grams	**4** grams

Summerberry smoothy

Serves 1

100g/3½oz frozen summer berries, partly defrosted

200ml/⅓ pint skimmed milk

intense sweetener to taste

A selection of smoothies

Place the berries and the milk in a food processor or blender and blend until smooth and frothy, sweeten to taste and serve.

PER SERVING

energy	protein	carbohydrate	fat
93 kcal	**7** grams	**16** grams	**0** grams

Kedgeree

Serves 2

100g/3½oz mix long grain and wild rice

100g/3½oz smoked haddock fillet, skinned

150ml/¼ pint skimmed milk

knob of butter

1 small onion, chopped

½ teaspoon curry powder (optional)

grated rind and juice ½ lemon

1 hard boiled egg, chopped

2 tablespoons fresh parsley, chopped

salt and freshly ground black pepper

Cook the rice according to the pack instructions. Drain. Place the haddock and the milk in a small saucepan, bring to the boil then simmer gently for 5 minutes until cooked through. Drain off the milk, then flake the fish.

Melt the butter in a non-stick pan, add the onion and fry for 2-3 minutes until softened. Stir in all the remaining ingredients, heat through, season well and serve.

PER SERVING

energy	protein	carbohydrate	fat
207 kcal	**13** grams	**32** grams	**3** grams

Fruity microwave porridge

Serves 2

3 tablespoons porridge oats

150ml/¼ pint skimmed milk

75g/2¾oz mixed dried fruit, eg chopped ready to eat apricots, sultanas

intense sweetener to taste

Place the oats and the milk in a microwavable dish, and cook on full power for 4-5 minutes, stirring half way through cooking time. Stir through the fruit and stand for 1 minute. Sweeten to taste.

For a change, stir a little cocoa powder through the milk before cooking and replace the dried fruit for a sliced banana.

PER SERVING			
energy	protein	carbohydrate	fat
199 kcal	**8** grams	**35** gram	**2** grams

Drop scones with blueberry topping

Makes 18 • Suitable for freezing

100g/3½oz self-raising flour

1 teaspoon ground mixed spice

2 tablespoons caster sugar

1 egg, beaten

150ml/¼ pint skimmed milk

a little oil for cooking

For the blueberry topping

150g/5½oz blueberries

Sift the flour and spice into a bowl then stir though the sugar, then make a well in the centre. Whisk together the egg and the milk, pour into the well in the flour and beat together to form a smooth batter.

Using kitchen paper wipe a little oil in the base of a non-stick frying pan. Drop spoonfuls of the mixture into the pan and cook for 2-3 minutes on each side, until golden. Continue until the mixture is all used up.

Meanwhile, place the blueberries in small pan and heat gently until they soften and become juicy. Serve the drop scones topped with some blueberries.

PER DROP SCONE			
energy	protein	carbohydrate	fat
110 kcal	**4** grams	**22** grams	**1** grams

Ham, spring onion and tomato omelette

Serves 1

2 eggs

1 tablespoon milk

1 tablespoon fresh mixed herbs, chopped

a little oil for frying

25g/1oz lean ham, chopped

2 spring onions, chopped

1 tomato, chopped

salt and freshly ground black pepper

In a bowl whisk together the eggs, milk and herbs. Season well. Very lightly brush a small non-stick pan with a little oil. Heat the pan then add the egg mixture, gently bring the sides toward the middle of the pan allowing any liquid egg run to the edges to cook. When almost set add the ham, spring onions and tomato. Fold the omelette in half, then transfer to a serving plate and serve immediately with fresh wholemeal toast.

PER SERVING			
energy	protein	carbohydrate	fat
225 kcal	**20** grams	**5** grams	**12** grams

Ham, spring onion and tomato omelette

Spiced grilled banana sandwich

Serves 1

2 slices, fruit and nut loaf

1 banana, mashed

pinch ground cinnamon

1 teaspoon maple syrup

Preheat the grill to high. Toast the fruit loaf on one side, spread the banana onto the untoasted sides of the bread and sprinkle over the cinnamon, drizzle over the syrup and place under the grill for 1-2 minutes until golden and bubbling.

PER SERVING

energy	protein	carbohydrate	fat
327 kcal	**7** grams	**67** grams	**6** grams

Crunchy homemade muesli

Enough for a portion every day of the week. Much tastier than a shop bought variety and cheaper too.

Makes 7 portions

200g/7oz jumbo porridge oats

25g/1oz toasted sunflower seeds

25g/1oz flaked almonds, toasted

75g/2¾oz ready to eat dried apricots, roughly chopped

75g/2¾oz sultanas

25g/1oz shredded coconut, toasted

Simply combine together all the ingredients serve and store in an airtight container.

PER SERVING

energy	protein	carbohydrate	fat
204 kcal	**6** grams	**33** grams	**6** grams

Bagels

As a change to toast why not try a bagel, delicious simply toasted with a little jam or follow the topping ideas below. Try different types of bagel such as cinnamon and raisin, plain or a savoury one such as onion.

Feeling fruity
Spread a little extra light cream cheese over a toasted bagel and topped with sliced fresh fruit, eg strawberries, banana and mango.

Simply savoury
Spread a little extra light cream cheese over a toasted bagel and top with sliced tomatoes and chopped spring onion.

Sunday special
Mix together a little extra light cream cheese and a little lemon juice and spread over a toasted bagel, top with a little smoked salmon and chopped chives.

"...can be **interesting** as well as **quick to prepare**"

Light meals

Regular meals are essential to achieving good blood glucose control and helping in the battle of the bulge.

Lunch may often be pushed aside due to rushing around for the children, working to tight deadlines or just due to countless errands to be run.

Even if you don't take any diabetes medication at lunchtime, you still need to fit in lunch to achieve a balanced food intake across the day.

Lunch is not to be missed and can be interesting as well as quick to prepare.

Grab the opportunity to include more fruit and veg: add salad or veg to your sandwich and fill up on fruit for dessert.

Italian bread salad

Delicious Mediterranean flavours combined in this tasty salad.

Serves 2

½ ciabatta loaf, torn into bite-sized pieces

¼ cucumber, chopped

3 tomatoes, chopped

1 small red onion, sliced

8 black olives

15g/½oz pinenuts toasted

2 tablespoons lemon and herb dressing (see page 56)

handful basil leaves, torn

Place the bread pieces under a preheated grill and cook for 2-3 minutes until lightly toasted all over. Place in a salad bowl and toss in the remaining ingredients. Leave for 30 minutes, to allow the flavours to develop. Serve.

PER SERVING			
energy	protein	carbohydrate	fat
325 kcal	**9** grams	**44** grams	**14** grams

Warm smoked mackerel salad

Serves 1

125g/4½oz new potatoes, scrubbed

2 tablespoons fat free French dressing

75g/2¾oz French beans, halved

small bunch watercress

6 cherry tomatoes, halved

100g/3½oz peppered smoked mackerel fillet, flaked

1 egg, poached

Cook the potatoes in a pan of boiling water for 10-12 minutes until tender. Drain and toss through the dressing. Cool. Mix together the potatoes, beans, watercress, tomatoes and mackerel and tip into a serving dish. Top with a poached egg and serve.

Italian bread salad

PER SERVING

energy	protein	carbohydrate	fat
401 kcal	**21** grams	**30** grams	**18** grams

Baked sweet potato with chilli fromage frais filling

Serves 2

2 medium sized sweet potatoes

1 tablespoon oil

1 red chilli, finely chopped

1 clove garlic, crushed

1 onion, finely chopped

2 tablespoons fresh coriander, chopped

3 tablespoons virtually fat free fromage frais

2 tablespoons light crème fraîche

Preheat the oven to 200°C/400°F/gas mark 6. Prick the sweet potatoes all over, and place in the oven and cook for 1-1¼ hours until tender.

Meanwhile, heat the oil in a pan, add the chilli, garlic and onion and fry for 3-4 minutes until softened. Remove from the heat and stir in the remaining ingredients.

Make a cross in the potatoes, squeeze open and spoon in the filling. Serve with plenty of salad.

PER SERVING

energy	protein	carbohydrate	fat
284 kcal	**9** grams	**44** grams	**9** grams

Stuffed tortillas

Tortillas are a type of unleavened bread, which provide an alternative form of starchy carbohydrate with a meal.

Serves 2

1 teaspoon olive oil
1 onion, chopped
1 red pepper, sliced
1 boneless, skinless, chicken breast, sliced
1 x 400g can red kidney beans, drained and rinsed
1 tablespoon light crème fraîche
3 small flour tortillas
1 carrot, peeled and grated
1 x 60g bag mixed salad leaves
salt and freshly ground black pepper

Heat the oil in a non-stick frying pan add the onion and red pepper and fry for 2-3 minutes, until softened. Add the chicken and fry for 3-4 minutes until browned and cooked through. In a bowl mash together the kidney beans and crème fraîche. Divide the bean mixture between the tortillas, spoon over the chicken mixture, add the carrot and salad leaves. Season well, roll up, cut in half and serve.

> **NUTRITION TIP**
>
> Fill up on a variety of different breads to provide carbohydrate with meals, but make sure you don't add extra fat.

PER SERVING

energy	protein	carbohydrate	fat
512 kcal	**38** grams	**82** grams	**6** grams

Spicy butternut squash soup

Serves 4 • Suitable for freezing

1 tablespoon olive oil

1 onion, chopped

1 red chilli, chopped (optional)

1 clove garlic, crushed

2 butternut squash, flesh cubed

1 tablespoon medium curry paste

300ml(½ pints) good vegetable stock

200ml (7fl oz) coconut milk

2 tablespoons fresh coriander, chopped

Heat the oil in a non-stick pan. Add the onion, chilli and the garlic, and fry for 4-5 minutes until softened. Add the squash and continue to fry for 5 minutes. Stir through the curry paste and fry for a further minute. Pour over the stock, bring to the boil, cover and simmer for 15-20 minutes, until the squash is tender. Transfer to a food processor or blender and blend until smooth. Return to the pan, add the coconut milk and coriander then season well. Serve with plenty of crusty bread.

> **NUTRITION TIP**
>
> Although coconut milk contains a rich source of saturated fat, the amount per serving is quite small.

PER SERVING

energy	protein	carbohydrate	fat
89 kcal	**1** gram	**13** grams	**4** grams

Saag aloo (spinach & potatoes)

Serves 2

1 tablespoon olive oil

1 small onion, finely chopped

2 cloves garlic, finely chopped

1 green chilli

1 teaspoon chopped ginger

Butternut soup

½ teaspoon turmeric

450g/1lb potatoes peeled and cut into small pieces

½ teaspoon red chilli powder

225g/8oz spinach leaves, finely chopped

Heat oil in a non-stick frying pan, add the onion, garlic, chilli and ginger and cook for 2-3 minutes until softened. Stir in the turmeric and cook for 5 minutes. Add the potatoes and red chilli powder, stir, cover and cook for 10-15 minutes over a medium heat.

Stir through the spinach, cover and cook for 25-30 minutes, until the potatoes are tender and the mixture quite dry.

Serve with boiled rice or chapati.

NUTRITION TIP

Spinach is an excellent source of beta carotene (the plant form of vitamin A) and a good source of vitamins C and folate. A colourful leaf vegetable commonly used in many Asian foods, either, fresh or frozen.

PER SERVING

energy	protein	carbohydrate	fat
257 kcal	**8** grams	**43** grams	**6** grams

Muttar pilau (rice with peas)

Serves 3

1 tablespoon olive oil

½ small onion finely sliced

1 clove garlic finely chopped

1 teaspoon chopped ginger

1 teaspoon garam masala powder

75g/2¾oz frozen or fresh peas

2 tablespoons low fat natural yogurt

250g/9oz Basmati rice, washed and soaked for 30 minutes to 1 hour, then drained

½ teaspoon black cumin seeds

Heat the oil in a non-stick pan. Add the onion and fry for 8-10 minutes until golden brown. Pour over 150ml/¼pint water, bring to the boil, cover and simmer for 5 minutes. Stir, then add the garlic, ginger and garam masala, cook for 30 seconds then add the peas, yogurt and 450ml/¾ pint of water. Bring to the boil, then add the rice and cumin seeds. Mix well, then cover and cook for 10 to 15 minutes over a low heat, until the rice is tender and the liquid has been absorbed. Leave for 5 minutes, then serve.

PER SERVING			
energy	protein	carbohydrate	fat
370 kcal	**10** grams	**72** grams	**4** grams

Channa dahl (yellow lentils)

Serves 4

225g/8oz yellow lentils washed and soaked for 2 hours

½ teaspoon red chilli powder

2 cloves of garlic, chopped

¼ teaspoon tumeric

1 tablespoon olive or sunflower oil

1 small onion, sliced

1 green chilli, finely chopped

½ teaspoon garam masala powder

1 tablespoon fresh coriander chopped

Put the water in the pan, enough to cover the lentils (plus 1½ inches above). Add the chilli powder, garlic, tumeric and half of the oil and bring to the boil. Drain the channa dahl and mix thoroughly. Place on the lid, and cook for approximately an hour on a medium heat, until tender and mixed so it's not too thick.

Heat the remaining oil in a frying pan, add the sliced onion and cook until golden brown, then add green chilli. Add all of the ingredients to the pan with the dahl and sprinkle with garam masala and fresh coriander.

Serve with boiled rice or chapati.

PER SERVING

energy	protein	carbohydrate	fat
236 kcal	**15** grams	**38** grams	**3** grams

Chilli bean soup with tomato salsa

Serves 6 • Suitable for freezing

1 tablespoon oil

1 large onion, chopped

2 cloves garlic, crushed

2 red chillies, finely chopped

1 teaspoon ground cumin

1/2 teaspoon ground cinnamon

2 x 400g cans kidney beans, drained and rinsed

1 x 400g can chopped tomatoes

900ml/1 1/2 pint vegetable stock

For the salsa

2 tomatoes, finely chopped

4 tablespoon fresh coriander, chopped

1/2 small red onion, finely chopped

salt and freshly ground black pepper

Heat the oil in a large pan, add the onion, garlic and chillies and fry for 2-3 minutes until the onion begins to soften. Add the spices and continue to fry for a further minute. Add the remaining soup ingredients to the pan, bring to the boil, cover and simmer for 20 minutes. Transfer the soup to a food processor or blender and process until smooth (it may be easier to do this in batches), return to the pan and heat through. Meanwhile, mix together all the ingredients for the salsa.

Serve the soup topped with a spoonful of salsa and with tortillas or flat-bread.

PER SERVING			
energy	protein	carbohydrate	fat
129 kcal	**8** grams	**23** grams	**1** gram

Minestrone

Serves 6 • Suitable for freezing

1 teaspoon oil

2 cloves garlic, crushed

1 large onion, chopped

1 large carrot, chopped

2 sticks celery, finely sliced

450g/1lb floury potatoes, chopped

1.5L/2¾ pints vegetable stock

1 x 400g can chopped tomatoes

125g/4½oz pasta shapes

200g/7oz French beans, halved

100g/3½oz frozen peas

¼ Savoy cabbage, roughly chopped

4 tablespoons fresh parsley, chopped

3 teaspoons pesto sauce

2 tablespoons fresh parmesan shavings

salt and freshly ground pepper

Heat the oil in a large pan, add the garlic, onion, carrot, celery and potatoes and fry for 3-4 minutes until beginning to soften but not brown. Add the stock and tomatoes, bring to the boil and simmer for 10 minutes. Add the pasta, beans, peas and cabbage and continue to cook for a further 10 minutes, or until the pasta is cooked. Stir through the parsley and pesto and season well. Serve topped with shavings of parmesan and a traditional Italian bread such as ciabatta or foccacia.

PER SERVING

energy	protein	carbohydrate	fat
208 kcal	**9** grams	**36** grams	**4** grams

Salad dressings

A crisp green salad with dressing is ideal as a light lunch with bread. However, beware! Salad dressings and mayonnaise can be laden with fat and calories, try some of these ideas which are much lower in fat or some even fat free!

Red pepper and coriander dressing

2 red peppers, halved

1 tablespoon olive oil

1 teaspoon white wine vinegar

1 teaspoon caster sugar

2 tablespoons fresh coriander, chopped

2 tablespoons water

Grill the peppers, skin side up under a hot grill, until the skin is blackened. When cool remove the skin and place into a blender or food processor with all the remaining ingredients and blend until smooth. Serve.

TOTAL

energy	protein	carbohydrate	fat
280 kcal	**3** gram	**41** grams	**12** grams

Lemon and herb dressing

grated rind and juice 1 lemon

2 tablespoons olive oil

2 teaspoons caster sugar

2 teaspoon Dijon mustard

2 tablespoons mixed fresh herbs, chopped

Blend together all the ingredients in a blender or food processor. Serve.

TOTAL			
energy	protein	carbohydrate	fat
297 kcal	**1** gram	**21** grams	**22** grams

Creamy honey and mustard salad dressing

1 x 200g carton virtually fat free fromage frais

1 tablespoons wholegrain mustard

2 teaspoons runny honey

salt and freshly ground black pepper

Mix together all the ingredients and serve. Delicious spooned over grilled chicken salad (see page 62).

TOTAL			
energy	protein	carbohydrate	fat
204 kcal	**18** grams	**27** grams	**3** grams

Low fat dips

Shop bought dips can be high in fat. Try these as a delicious and healthy change.

Hummus

In a blender or food processor blend together 1 x 400g chickpeas (drained and rinsed), 1 clove garlic, grated rind and juice 1 lemon, 200g carton virtually fat free fromage frais and a pinch of paprika.

TOTAL energy	protein	carbohydrate	fat
461 kcal	**37** grams	**62** grams	**9** grams

Tzatziki

In a bowl mix together 1 x 200g carton virtually fat free fromage frais, ¼ cucumber finely chopped, 2 tablespoons mint chopped, 2 tablespoons parsley, chopped and 1 clove crushed garlic.

TOTAL energy	protein	carbohydrate	fat
121 kcal	**15** grams	**14** grams	**0** grams

Tomato salsa

In a blender or food processor, blend together 1 x 400g can chopped tomatoes, 1 red chilli, 1 clove garlic and 2 tablespoons fresh coriander.

TOTAL energy	protein	carbohydrate	fat
64 kcal	**4** grams	**12** grams	**0** grams

Tuna and chickpea pitta pockets

Serves 2

2 pitta bread

1 x 120g can tuna in water, drained

grated rind and juice ½ lime

1 tablespoon parsley, chopped

6 cherry tomatoes, chopped

¼ cucumber, chopped

½ can chickpeas, drained and rinsed

½ red onion, finely chopped

salt and freshly ground black pepper

Splash a little water onto the pitta breads then toast under a preheated grill for 1-2 minutes until, lightly browned and puffed up.

Mix together all the remaining ingredients and season well. Cut the pittas in half, then fill each half with the tuna mixture.

PER SERVING			
energy	protein	carbohydrate	fat
354 kcal	**24** grams	**60** grams	**4** grams

Baked stuffed mushrooms on toast

Serves 2

4 large field mushrooms

2 slices lean back bacon, chopped

1 clove garlic, crushed

100g/3½oz light cream cheese

2 tablespoons fresh parsley, chopped

75g/2¾oz sweetcorn, defrosted if frozen

salt and freshly ground black pepper

4 thick slices French bread

Preheat the oven to 200°C/400°F/gas mark 6.

Place the mushrooms into an ovenproof dish. Heat a non-stick frying pan add the bacon and garlic and fry for 2-3 minutes until beginning to crisp. Tip into bowl and mix together with the cream cheese, parsley and sweetcorn. Season well. Divide the mixture between the mushrooms. Cook for 25-30 minutes until the mushrooms are tender.

Toast the French bread on each side, then top each piece of bread with a mushroom.

PER SERVING			
energy	protein	carbohydrate	fat
268 kcal	**13** grams	**40** grams	**7** grams

Roasted vegetable and bulgar wheat salad

Serves 2

1 courgette, halved lengthways and cut into wedges

1 red pepper cut into chunks

1 red onion, cut into wedges

1 small aubergine, cut into chunks

8 cherry tomatoes

oil for drizzling

10 black olives

125g/4$\frac{1}{2}$oz bulgar wheat

1 tablespoon olive oil

grated rind and juice 1 orange

1 tablespoon balsamic vinegar

3 tablespoons fresh mixed herbs, eg basil, parsley, oregano, chopped

Preheat the grill to high. Place the courgette, pepper, onion and aubergine on a foil lined baking sheet and drizzle over the oil. Place under the grill and cook for 7-8 minutes until almost tender and beginning to char. Add the tomatoes and olives and continue to cook for 2 minutes.

Meanwhile, soak the bulgar wheat according to the pack instructions. Toss together all the ingredients including the vegetables and serve. Also delicious served cold.

PER SERVING			
energy	protein	carbohydrate	fat
220 kcal	**6** grams	**30** grams	**9** grams

Griddled chicken salad

Serves 2

1 large boneless, skinless chicken breast
grated rind and juice 1 orange
1 tablespoon wholegrain mustard
250g/9oz new potatoes, halved
1 teaspoon olive oil
large bunch watercress
3 spring onions, sliced
¼ cucumber, chopped

Place the chicken in a non-metallic bowl. Mix together the orange and mustard, pour over the chicken and leave to marinate for 20 minutes. Cook the potatoes in boiling water until tender. Drain.

Brush the griddle pan with the oil then heat until very hot, remove the chicken from the marinade, place on the griddle and cook for 6-7 minutes each side, until cooked through. Pour over the marinade and heat through. Slice the chicken then toss together with all the other ingredients.

Serve with extra bread if desired.

PER SERVING			
energy	protein	carbohydrate	fat
220 kcal	**27** grams	**20** grams	**4** grams

Lamb kebab in pitta with salsa

Serves 2

1 small onion, grated

150g/5$\frac{1}{2}$oz lean minced lamb

pinch paprika

pinch cumin

pinch dried chilli flakes

1 tablespoon fresh coriander, chopped

For the salsa

$\frac{1}{2}$ red onion, sliced

$\frac{1}{4}$ cucumber, halved and sliced

1 tomato, chopped

1 tablespoon fresh coriander, chopped

To serve

2 pitta bread

lettuce leaves, shredded

2 tablespoons virtually fat free fromage frais

Place the onion, lamb, paprika, cumin, chilli and coriander in a bowl and combine well. Form the mixture around 4 wooden skewers. Place under a preheated grill and grill for 4-5 minutes until browned and cooked through.

Mix together the ingredients for the salsa. Splash the pittas with a little water and toast under the grill for 1-2 minutes until golden and puffed up. Stuff the pittas with a little lettuce, the lamb from the skewers and top with the salsa and a spoon of fromage frais.

PER SERVING			
energy	protein	carbohydrate	fat
365 kcal	**22** grams	**51** grams	**9** grams

"...many people don't have **time** to prepare meals at **home**"

Main
meals

Most people still have one 'main' meal of the day. With increasingly busy lives, many people don't have time to prepare meals at home. We've included a selection of quick and easy recipes to give maximum taste with minimum fat and fuss.

If you are used to cooking meals for yourself and your family, this should provide you with plenty of fresh ideas to incorporate into your everyday meal planning. Main meals when you are slimming will usually be one course with fruit or low calorie yogurt to finish.

When entertaining, meals tend to be higher in fat and therefore extra calories. Special occasion meals do not 'ruin' a weight reducing diet. However, if you entertain more often or cater for people trying to lose weight, you need to think about the choices you make.

Cod with red pepper and spinach sauce

Serves 2

½ x 400g can pimentoes, drained

1 clove garlic, crushed

1 teaspoon caster sugar

2 tablespoons light crème fraîche

pinch grated nutmeg

2 pieces thick cod fillet (each weighing approx 150g/5½oz)

125g/4½oz baby spinach

salt and freshly ground black pepper

Place the pimentoes, garlic, sugar, crème fraîche and nutmeg into a food processor or blender and blend until smooth. Pour into a medium saucepan, place the cod on top. Bring to the boil, cover and simmer gently for 6-7 minutes until the fish is just cooked. Stir through the spinach and cook until wilted. Season well. Serve with new potatoes and vegetables.

PER SERVING			
energy	protein	carbohydrate	fat
217 kcal	**31** grams	**12** grams	**5** grams

Marinated chicken with lentil salad

Serves 2

2 boneless, skinless chicken breasts

1 clove garlic, crushed

1 tablespoon wholegrain mustard

grated rind and juice 1 lemon

2 teaspoons runny honey

3 tablespoons fresh parsley, chopped

2 tomatoes, chopped

2 spring onions, chopped

2 tablespoons fat free French dressing

150g/5½oz tinned green lentils, drained

Cod with red pepper and spinach sauce

Make 3 slashes across each chicken breast and place in a non-metallic bowl. Mix together the garlic, mustard, lemon juice and honey, pour over the chicken and leave to marinate for at least 30 minutes. Mix together the remaining ingredients and set aside. Cook the chicken under a hot grill basting occasionally with the marinade. Serve with the lentil mixture.

PER SERVING			
energy	protein	carbohydrate	fat
277 kcal	**40** grams	**22** grams	**3** grams

Thai chicken stir-fry

Serves 2

1 teaspoon sunflower oil

2 chicken breasts, thinly sliced

2 cloves garlic, sliced

2.5cm/1 inch fresh ginger, peeled and grated

1 red chilli, finely sliced

1 bunch spring onions, sliced

1 red pepper, seeded and cubed

grated rind and juice of 1 lime

1 tablespoon runny honey

large bunch basil

1 tablespoon reduced salt soy sauce

Heat the oil in a frying pan or wok, until beginning to smoke. Add the chicken and fry for 2-3 minutes until golden, remove from the pan with a slotted spoon and set aside.

Add the garlic, ginger and chilli and fry for a minute, add the spring onions and pepper and continue to fry for 2 minutes. Return the chicken to the pan with the remaining ingredients and heat through, until piping hot. Serve with rice or noodles.

NUTRITION TIP

Unlike this recipe many Thai dishes use coconut milk which is high in saturated fat.

PER SERVING			
energy	protein	carbohydrate	fat
195 kcal	**33** grams	**7** grams	**4** grams

Moroccan style chicken

Serve this dish with couscous – a traditional North African staple. Alternative starchy carbohydrates like this add variety to main meals.

Serves 2

2 cinnamon sticks

2 large skinless chicken thighs

1 cloves garlic, crushed

1 teaspoon paprika

$\frac{1}{2}$ teaspoon cumin

1 teaspoon olive oil

1 carrot, chopped

75g/2$\frac{3}{4}$oz French beans, halved

$\frac{1}{2}$ teaspoon tumeric

25g/1oz green olives

50g/1$\frac{3}{4}$oz ready-to-eat dried apricots

grated rind and juice of $\frac{1}{2}$ lemon

200ml/7fl oz chicken stock

1 tablespoon fresh mint chopped, plus a little to garnish

salt and freshly ground black pepper

Wrap each chicken thigh around a cinnamon stick. Mix together the garlic, paprika, cumin and half the oil. Place the chicken pieces into a non-metallic dish, spoon over the spice mixture and coat, then leave to marinate for at least 1 hour.

Heat the remaining oil in a pan, add the chicken pieces (still wrapped around the cinnamon stick) and brown all over. Remove from the pan using a slotted spoon and set aside. Add the carrot and beans to the pan, cook over a low heat for about 5-6 minutes. Stir in the tumeric, then add all the remaining ingredients (except the stock) to the pan, along with the chicken. Pour over 200ml/7fl oz stock, bring to the boil cover and simmer for 12-15 minutes, until the chicken is tender. Season and garnish with mint.

PER SERVING

energy	protein	carbohydrate	fat
275 kcal	**27** grams	**13** grams	**12** grams

Mediterranean vegetable pasta

Serves 2

175g/6oz dried pasta shapes

1 tablespoon olive oil

1 red pepper, sliced

1 courgette, sliced

1 small onion, sliced

1 clove garlic, crushed

100g/3½oz cherry tomatoes, halved

½ x 400g tin artichoke hearts, drained and halved

1 tablespoon pinenuts, toasted

handful fresh basil, torn

salt and freshly ground black pepper

Cook the pasta according to the pack instructions. Drain.

Meanwhile, heat the oil in a non-stick frying pan. Add the pepper, courgette, onion and garlic and fry for 4-5 minutes, until softened. Add the tomatoes and artichoke hearts and continue to fry for 1-2 minutes until warmed through. Toss together all the remaining ingredients, including the pasta, season well and serve.

PER SERVING

energy	protein	carbohydrate	fat
472 kcal	**16** grams	**79** grams	**11** grams

Mediterranean vegetable pasta

Singapore style hearty noodle broth

Serves 3

1 teaspoon oil

1 chicken breast, thinly sliced

$^1/_2$ red pepper, sliced

2 tablespoons Thai curry paste (available in most supermarkets in the herb and spice section)

1 x 400g can reduced fat coconut milk

250g pack cooked noodles, eg rice noodles, udon noodles

75g/2$^3/_4$oz mangetout, halved

75g/2$^3/_4$oz beansprouts

1 bunch spring onions, chopped

50g/1$^3/_4$oz cooked peeled prawns (optional)

2 tablespoons fresh coriander, chopped

Heat the oil in a non-stick pan. Add the chicken and pepper and fry for 2 minutes. Add the Thai curry paste and continue to fry for 2 minutes. Pour in the coconut milk and simmer for 1 minute. Stir in all the remaining ingredients and simmer for 2 minutes. Serve in large bowls with some crusty bread.

PER SERVING			
energy	protein	carbohydrate	fat
358 kcal	**22** grams	**53** grams	**6** grams

Spaghetti with chilli, tomato and bacon

Serves 3

225g/8oz spaghetti

1 teaspoon olive oil

1 clove garlic, crushed

1 red chilli, finely chopped

100g/3$^1/_2$oz lean back bacon, chopped

300ml/$^1/_2$ pint passata (sieved tomotoes)

2 tablespoons fresh parsley, chopped

Cook the spaghetti according to the pack instructions. Drain and return to the pan.

Meanwhile, heat the oil in a non-stick pan, add the garlic, chilli and bacon and fry for 3-4 minutes until the bacon begins to crisp. Add the passata, bring to the boil and simmer for 5 minutes.

Mix the sauce through the pasta with the parsley and serve with salad.

PER SERVING			
energy	protein	carbohydrate	fat
448 kcal	**14** grams	**41** grams	**7** grams

Ginger, garlic and orange lamb fillet

Serves 2

200g/7oz piece lean lamb fillet, cut into thick slices

1cm/½inch piece fresh ginger, peeled and grated

2 cloves garlic, crushed

grated rind and juice 1 orange

1 teaspoon oil

3 tablespoons fresh coriander, chopped

Place the lamb fillet into a non-metallic bowl with the ginger, garlic and orange rind and juice. Set aside for at least 30 minutes.

Heat the oil in a non-stick frying pan. Remove the lamb from the marinade (reserving the marinade), add to the pan and fry for 2-3 minutes until golden. Add the marinade and the coriander, heat through and serve with new potatoes and vegetables.

PER SERVING			
energy	protein	carbohydrate	fat
229 kcal	**19** grams	**3** grams	**14** grams

Mixed fish steamed parcels with herbed salsa

Serves 2

150g/5$\frac{1}{2}$oz boneless, skinless salmon fillet, cubed

150g/5$\frac{1}{2}$oz boneless, skinless cod fillet, cubed

4 scallops

grated rind and juice 1 lime

salt and freshly ground black pepper

For the salsa

3 spring onions, chopped

2 tablespoons mixed fresh herbs, chopped eg. Parsley, oregano

100g/3$\frac{1}{2}$oz cucumber, chopped

3 tablespoons virtually fat free fromage frais

Cut 2 squares of baking parchment, approx 25 x 25cm, divide the fish and scallops between the 2 squares and drizzle over the lime rind and juice and season well. Fold up the parcels and secure. Place in a steamer and steam for 8-10 minutes until the fish is cooked.

Meanwhile, mix together all the ingredients for the salsa and serve with the fish, along with potatoes and plenty of vegetables or salad.

Note: if you do not have a steamer then preheat the oven to 200°C/400°F/gas mark 6. Half fill a roasting tin with boiling water, lay a wire rack over the roasting tin and place the parcels on the rack. Cook in the oven for 10-12 minutes or until the fish is cooked.

Serve with a starchy carbohydrate like rice or potatoes and plenty of vegetables or salad.

PER SERVING			
energy	protein	carbohydrate	fat
290 kcal	**43** grams	**8** grams	**8** grams

Tofu kebabs with Oriental stir-fried vegetables

Serves 2

1/2 x 285g pack tofu	
2 tablespoons soy sauce	
2 tablespoons oyster sauce	
1 clove garlic, crushed	
1 red pepper, cut into chunks	
1 small onion, cut into wedges	

For the stir-fry

1 teaspoon oil	
1 pak choi (like a Chinese lettuce), chopped	
100g/3½oz beansprouts	
2 spring onions, sliced	
2 tablespoons fresh coriander, chopped	

Place the tofu in a non-metallic bowl. Mix together the soy sauce, oyster sauce and the garlic, pour over the tofu and leave to marinate for at least 1 hour, preferably overnight. Remove the tofu from the marinade (reserving the marinade), thread onto kebab sticks with the pepper and onions. Heat the grill to high and grill the kebabs for 7-8 minutes until cooked and golden.

Meanwhile, heat the oil in a non-stick frying pan and add the remaining stir-fry ingredients and fry for 2-3 minutes until just cooked. Pour over the reserved marinade and heat through, serve with the kebabs and plenty of freshly cooked noodles.

PER SERVING

energy	protein	carbohydrate	fat
159 kcal	**11** grams	**19** grams	**4** grams

Lemon and herb chicken with chickpeas

Serves 2

2 boneless, skinless chicken breasts (approx 125g/4½oz each)
grated rind and juice 1 lemon
1 clove garlic, crushed
pinch turmeric
1 teaspoon olive oil
1 teaspoon black mustard seeds
1 teaspoon cumin seeds
4 spring onions, chopped
1 x 400g chickpeas, drained and rinsed
3 tablespoons mixed fresh herbs, chopped, eg coriander, parsley
2 tablespoons light crème fraîche
salt and freshly ground black pepper

Place the chicken in a non-metallic dish add the garlic, turmeric, lemon rind and juice. Combine and set aside for 30 minutes.

Heat the oil in a non-stick frying pan add the mustard seeds and the cumin seeds and fry for 1 minute until fragrant. Add the chicken to the pan and fry for 2 minutes on each side. Add the marinade to the pan along with 100ml/3½ fl oz water, cover and simmer for 7-8 minutes, turning occasionally until cooked through. Add the remaining ingredients, cook for a further 2 minutes, season well and serve will bread and salad.

PER SERVING

energy	protein	carbohydrate	fat
397 kcal	**54** grams	**26** grams	**9** grams

Lemon and herb chicken with chickpeas

Mediterranean fish stew

Serves 2

1 teaspoon olive oil

1 small onion, chopped

1 clove garlic, crushed

1 stick celery, chopped

300g/10 1/2 oz potatoes, chopped

1 x 200g can chopped tomatoes

1 tablespoon fresh herbs, chopped

1 bay leaf

grated rind 1 lemon

150ml/1/4 pint fish stock

200g/7oz boneless, skinless cod fillet, cubed

100g/3 1/2 oz prawns, defrosted if frozen

Heat the oil in a pan, add the onion, garlic, celery and potato and fry for 4-5 minutes, until beginning to soften. Add the tomatoes, herbs, bay leaf, lemon rind and stock. Bring to the boil and simmer for 10 minutes. Add the cod and continue to cook for 7-8 minutes, adding the prawns 1 minute before the end of cooking time. Serve with plenty of vegetables and extra bread if wanted.

PER SERVING

energy	protein	carbohydrate	fat
236 kcal	**30** grams	**22** grams	**3** grams

Subhzee salun (mixed vegetable curry)

Serves 2

1 tablespoon olive oil

1 medium onion, sliced

2 cloves of garlic, chopped

1 teaspoon fresh ginger, chopped

2 tomatoes chopped

2 green chillies

1 teaspoon chilli powder

1 teaspoon coriander powder

450g/1lb mixed vegetables, eg carrots, peas, broad beans

350/12oz new potatoes peeled and cut into small pieces

1 tablespoon fresh coriander leaves

$\frac{1}{2}$ teaspoon garam masala powder

Heat the oil in a pan, add the onion, garlic and ginger and fry for 4 to 5 minutes until golden. Add the tomatoes, chilli, chilli powder and coriander powder, mix well and leave for 5 minutes. Stir through the vegetables and potatoes and cook gently for 30-35 minutes until the vegetables and potatoes are tender, and most of the liquid has evaporated. Garnish with the coriander and garam masala and serve with rice or naan.

PER SERVING			
energy	protein	carbohydrate	fat
330 kcal	**11** grams	**57** grams	**7** grams

Ghost salun (meat curry)

Serves 4 • Suitable for freezing

1 tablespoon olive or sunflower oil

2 medium sized onions, finely chopped

2 cloves of garlic chopped

1 tablespoon of chopped ginger

1 large tomato, skinned and chopped

$\frac{1}{2}$ teaspoon tumeric

1 teaspoon chilli powder

1 tablespoon coriander powder

450g/1lb lean lamb, cubed

3 tablespoons low fat natural yogurt

150ml/$\frac{1}{4}$pint water

1 teaspoon garam masala powder

1 tablespoon fresh coriander leaves

Heat the oil in a pan, add the onions, garlic and ginger and fry until soft and golden. Add the tomato, tumeric, chilli and coriander powder, mix well and simmer for 10 minutes. Stir through the meat and yogurt. Bring to the boil, cover and simmer for 1 hour, or until the meat is tender. Stir through the water and cook for a further 10 minutes.

Garnish with garam masala and coriander. Delicious served with muttar pilau (see page 52) or naan.

PER SERVING			
energy	protein	carbohydrate	fat
316 kcal	**24** grams	**12** grams	**17** grams

Grilled polenta with vegetable topping

Serves 2

For the polenta

500ml/18fl oz vegetable stock

125g/4½oz quick cook polenta

1 tablespoon fresh Parmesan, grated

knob of butter

2 tablespoons fresh parsley, chopped

For the vegetables

1 courgette, cut into chunks

½ medium aubergine, chopped

1 small red onion, sliced

2 tablespoons water

100g/3½oz mixed mushrooms, sliced

2 plum tomatoes, cut into chunks

1 tablespoon tomato purée

2 teaspoons pesto

salt and freshly ground black pepper

Bring the stock to the boil. In a steady stream, pour in the polenta and cook for 1 minute, or according to the pack instructions, until thickened. Stir in the remaining polenta ingredients, season well then tip out onto a baking sheet and spread to a square 2cm thick. Set aside until firm. Cut into 6 triangles, then place on a baking sheet and cook under a preheated grill for 2-3 minutes on each side until golden.

Meanwhile, heat a non-stick frying pan add the courgette, aubergine, onion and 2 tablespoons water and stir-fry for 3-4 minutes. Add the mushrooms and continue to cook for 3-4 minutes. Add the tomatoes, tomato purée, and the pesto heat for 2 minutes then season to taste. Serve the vegetables on the polenta.

PER SERVING

energy	protein	carbohydrate	fat
372 kcal	**16** grams	**55** grams	**9** grams

Griddled salmon

Serves 2

2 pieces boneless, skinless salmon fillet (approx 100g/3½oz each)

grated rind a juice 1 lime

1cm/½ inch piece ginger, grated

1 tablespoon soy sauce

2 tablespoons fresh coriander, chopped

Place the salmon fillets into a non-metallic bowl. Mix together the remaining ingredients and pour over the salmon, leave to marinate for at least 30 minutes.

Heat a griddle until very hot, remove the salmon from the marinate and place onto the griddle and cook for 3 minutes on each side. Pour over the marinade, heat through and serve with new potatoes and salad.

NUTRITION TIP

Marinades help to add flavour to low fat foods. Any meat, fish or bean curd (tofu) can be marinated before grilling, baking or steaming.

PER SERVING

energy	protein	carbohydrate	fat
185 kcal	**20** grams	**0** grams	**11** grams

" Choose fruit whether it's fresh, stewed or tinned "

Simply desserts

'Dessert', 'pudding', 'afters', whichever name you use, are traditionally calorie laden, high fat, high sugar dishes. But consumer trends are on the move - rich puddings on a daily basis are out and healthier options are in.

This change in approach means you needn't miss out simply because you have diabetes or are watching your weight. Desserts can be nutritious and still satisfy that need for something sweet at the end of a meal.

Choose fruit, whether it's fresh, stewed or tinned in juice and take advantage of this ideal time to boost your fruit intake.

Another fast and convenient low fat dessert is yogurt. Often, dieters mistakenly cut down on dairy foods, but milk and milk products can make a large contribution to your total calcium intake.

Choose 'low fat' or 'low calorie' versions.

Hot pineapple with minty fromage frais

Serves 3

1 fresh pineapple, peeled, sliced and core removed

1 x 200g carton virtually fat free fromage frais

1 tablespoon runny honey

2 tablespoons fresh mint, chopped

Heat a griddle until really hot. Lay on the pineapple slices and cook for 2-3 minutes each side until lightly caramelized (it may be easier to do this in batches). Mix together the virtually fat free fromage frais, honey and mint and serve with the griddled pineapple.

PER SERVING

energy	protein	carbohydrate	fat
151 kcal	**6** grams	**39** grams	**0** grams

Tropical fruit frozen yogurt

Serves 4

1 x 500g bag frozen tropical fruits

1 x 500g carton Greek yogurt

Simply place all the ingredients into a food processor or blender and blend until smooth. Serve immediately or transfer to a freezerproof container and freeze until required.

PER SERVING

energy	protein	carbohydrate	fat
195 kcal	**8** grams	**15** grams	**10** grams

Kiwi sorbet

Freeze half a kiwi fruit. Then eat straight out of the skin. Fat free and fantastically tasty!

Ice-cream espresso

For a simple delicious treat, place a scoop of vanilla ice-cream into a cup of freshly made espresso and eat with a spoon.

Banoffee sundae

Serves 2

200g carton virtually fat free fromage frais

2 tablespoons toffee sauce

1 medium banana, sliced

15g/½oz plain chocolate, grated

Beat together the fromage frais and toffee sauce. Divide the banana between 2 small glass dishes or ramekins, top with the fromage frais mixture then sprinkle with some chocolate.

PER SERVING energy	protein	carbohydrate	fat
193 kcal	**15** grams	**25** grams	**3** grams

Simple mango and orange sorbet

Serves 4

1 x 400g can mango, drained and roughly chopped

grated rind and juice 2 oranges

Place the mango pieces onto a cling film lined tray and place in the freezer until frozen. Place the frozen mango and the orange rind and juice into a food processor or blender and blend until smooth. Serve immediately or transfer to a container and freeze until required.

PER SERVING

energy	protein	carbohydrate	fat
66 kcal	**0** grams	**17** grams	**0** grams

Summerberry crush

Serves 3

200g/7oz frozen mixed summer berries, defrosted

200g carton virtually fat free fromage frais

1 tablespoon caster sugar or intense sweetener to taste

25g/1oz Amerreti biscuits, lightly crushed

Gently fold together all the ingredients, and spoon into serving glasses.

PER SERVING

energy	protein	carbohydrate	fat
117 kcal	**6** grams	**22** grams	**1** gram

Summerberry crush

> " ...what could be more convienient than **snacking** on **fruit?** "

Snack
ideas

To stabilise your blood glucose levels, spread your carbohydrate intake over the day by having regular meals. For people on insulin or taking sulphonylureas, snacks between meals are particularly recommended to help spread this carbohydrate intake.

Even if you are trying to lose weight, snacking is not 'bad', as long as you snack carefully – and what could be more convenient than snacking on fruit?

Below are some ideas in addition to the recipes in this section.

- Fruit wedges, raw vegetable sticks, breadsticks or tortilla chips with dips. Salsas or reduced fat dips are a lower fat choice. Use fruit yogurt as a sweet dip.

- Fruit yogurts or fromage frais. Look for 'low fat', 'diet' or 'lite' versions.

- Home-made milk shakes made with semi-skimmed milk, low fat yogurt and fruit whizzed up in a liquidiser.

- Mini buns, bread muffins, slices of malt or fruit loaf, scones.

- Popcorn. Home popped corn can be sprinkled with a little sweetener or salt or flavoured with some chilli powder, paprika or celery salt.

Sun-dried tomato and rosemary bread

Serves 20 • Suitable for freezing

750g/1lb10oz strong plain flour
pinch of salt
pinch of sugar
½ tablespoon fresh rosemary, chopped
8 sun-dried tomatoes, those in oil, chopped
1 x 7g sachet easy-blend yeast
1 tablespoon olive oil
450ml/¾pint warm water
milk for brushing

Preheat the oven to 220°C/425°F/gas mark 7.

Sift together the flour, salt and sugar into a large bowl. Stir in the rosemary, sun-dried tomatoes and yeast.

Mix the oil with 450ml/¾ pint warm water, pour into the flour mixture and combine to form a soft dough.

Tip the dough onto a lightly floured surface and knead for 6 minutes until smooth and elastic. Place the dough in a lightly oiled bowl, cover with a damp cloth and leave to prove for about 1 hour until doubled in size.

Re-knead the dough for 3 minutes then divide in 2 and shape each into a large sausage, make a criss-cross on the top of each. Place each loaf on a baking sheet, cover and leave for 20 minutes, until doubled in size.

Brush the loaves with a little milk then cook in a preheated for 35 minutes or until hollow sounding when tapped.

Delicious served warm.

PER SERVING

energy	protein	carbohydrate	fat
142 kcal	**4** grams	**28** grams	**2** grams

Sun-dried tomato and rosemary bread

Banana and oat muffins

Makes 14 • Suitable for freezing

250g/9oz plain flour

75g/2¾oz rolled oats

1 tablespoon baking powder

¼ teaspoon grated nutmeg

2 medium bananas, mashed

1 egg, beaten

75g/2¾oz butter, melted

25g/1oz light muscavado sugar

175ml/6fl oz buttermilk

3 tablespoons runny honey

Preheat the oven to 200°C/400°F/gas mark 6.

In a large bowl mix together the flour, oats, baking powder and nutmeg.

Mix together all the remaining ingredients and fold through the flour until just combined.

Spoon into lightly greased and floured muffin tins and bake for about 20 minutes until risen and golden.

Cool in the tin for 10 minutes then serve.

NUTRITION TIP

For a change, substitute the banana with different fruits, eg raspberries, blueberries, blackberries or pear.

PER MUFFIN

energy	protein	carbohydrate	fat
160 kcal	**4** grams	**25** grams	**5** grams

Banana and date bars

Makes 14

175g/6oz stoned dates, chopped

100ml/4fl oz water

3 medium bananas, mashed

250g/9oz reduced fat spread

25g/1oz soft brown sugar

175g/6oz plain wholemeal flour

1 teaspoon baking powder

200g/7oz rolled oats

Preheat the oven to 180°C/350°F/gas mark 4.

Place the dates in a saucepan with the water and simmer for about 10 minutes until soft. Remove from the heat and stir in the bananas.

Melt the spread and sugar in a saucepan. Remove from the heat and stir in the flour, baking powder and rolled oats. Press half the mixture into the base of a lightly greased 18 x 27cm shallow tin. Spoon over the date and banana mixture. Sprinkle over the remaining oat mixture and press down lightly.

Bake for 30 minutes until golden. Cool for 10 minutes, cut into 16 bars then continue to cool on a wire rack.

PER BAR			
energy	protein	carbohydrate	fat
192 kcal	**4** grams	**28** grams	**7** grams

Menu plans

Entertaining

Special occasions and celebrations needn't ruin your efforts at weight management. Eating high fat, high calorie food on the odd occasion should not make a significant contribution to your overall energy intake. Here are some suggestions for entertaining at home, or to give friends or relatives ideas on what to cook without too many extra calories.

Breakfast

Kedgeree **or**	page 38
Bagels	page 43

Light meal

Lamb kebab with pitta **or**	page 63
Roasted bulgar wheat salad	page 61

Main Meal

Moroccan style chicken **or**	page 69
Grilled polenta with vegetable topping	page 80

Dessert

Summerberry crush **or** fruit	page 86

Moroccan style chicken

Menu plans

Sporty/busy schedule

If you have an active lifestyle or lead life at a hectic pace, you need fast healthy meals to keep up your energy levels. Here is a selection of ideas to suit you. The meals are quick to prepare and lunch is portable to be convenient when time is short.

Breakfast

Fruity microwave porridge **or**	page 38
Banana booster	page 36

Light meal

Tuna and chickpea pitta pockets **or**	page 58
Chilli bean soup with tomato salsa	page 54

Main meal

Spaghetti with chilli and bacon **or**	page 72
Mediterranean vegetable pasta	page 70

Chilli bean soup with tomato salsa

Menu plans

Fitting in with the family

There is no reason why you should have separate meals simply because you are trying to lose weight. Family meals can often be adapted to reduce the fat and calorie content. You can vary the proportions of food on your plate. Give yourself more vegetables and a smaller protein portion (see page 22). Here is a selection of ideas for everyday meals that should appeal to the whole family.

Breakfast

Crunchy homemade muesli **or**	page 42
Spiced grilled banana sandwich	page 42

Light meal

Channa dahl **or**	page 53
Grilled chicken salad	page 62

Main meal

Ghost salun (meat curry) **or**	page 79
Tofu kebabs with Oriental stir-fry vegetables	page 75

Channa Dahl (yellow lentils)

index

Main meals

Meat   page
Ghost Salun (meat curry)   79
Ginger, garlic and orange
lamb fillet   73
Spaghetti with chilli, tomato
and bacon   72

Chicken
Lemon and herb with
chickpeas   76
Marinated with lentil salad   66
Moroccan style   69
Singapore style hearty
noodle broth   72
Thai stir-fry   68

Fish
Cod with red pepper and
spinach sauce   66
Griddled salmon   81
Mixed steam parcels with
herbed salsa   74
Mediteranean fish stew   78

Vegetarian
Grilled polenta with
vegetable topping   80
Mediteranean vegetable
pasta   70
Subhzee salun (mixed
vegetable curry)   78
Tofu kebabs with Oriental
stir-fry vegetables   75

Desserts

        page
Banoffee sundae   85
Hot pineapple with minty
fromage frais   84
Ice-cream espresso   85
Kiwi sorbet   84
Simple mango and
orange sorbet   86
Summerberry crush   86
Tropical fruit frozen yogurt   85

Snacks

        page
Banana and date bars   93
Banana and oat muffins   92
Sun-dried tomato and
rosemary bread   90

Further information

The Diabetes UK Careline offers help and support on all aspects of diabetes. We provide a confidential service which takes general enquiries from people with diabetes, their carers and from healthcare professionals. Our trained staff can give you the latest information on topics such as care of your diabetes, blood glucose levels, diet, illness, pregnancy, insurance, driving, welfare benefits and employment.

If you would like further information on any aspect of diabetes telephone or write to Diabetes UK Careline:

10 Parkway, London NW1 7AA

Telephone 020 7424 1030
(operates Language Line, for non-English speaking callers)

Textphone 020 7424 1031

Email careline@diabetes.org.uk

Further Diabetes UK cookbooks
- Everyday cookery - healthy recipes for the older person (2021) £4.95

- Creative recipes for all occasions (2025) £4.95

- Festive foods and easy entertaining (2027) £4.95

The Diabetes UK *Catalogue* descibes our full range of books and leaflets. For copies of this and other Diabetes UK leaflets, please contact:

Diabetes UK, Distribution Department, PO Box 3030, Swindon, Wiltshire SN3 4WN

Telephone 0800 585088

Diabetes UK national and regional offices

Diabetes UK is active at a national and regional level.

Diabetes UK, Central Office
London: 020 7424 1000

Diabetes UK North West
Warrington: 01925 653281

Diabetes UK West Midlands
Walsall: 01922 614500

Diabetes UK Northern & Yorkshire
Darlington: 01325 488606

Diabetes UK Northern Ireland
Belfast: 028 9066 6646

Diabetes UK Scotland
Glasgow: 0141 332 2700

Diabetes UK Cymru
Cardiff: 029 2066 8276

Diabetes UK

The charity for people with diabetes

10 Parkway, London NW1 7AA
Telephone 020 7424 1000 **Fax** 020 7424 1001
Email info@diabetes.org.uk **Website** www.diabetes.org.uk
Registered charity no. 215199